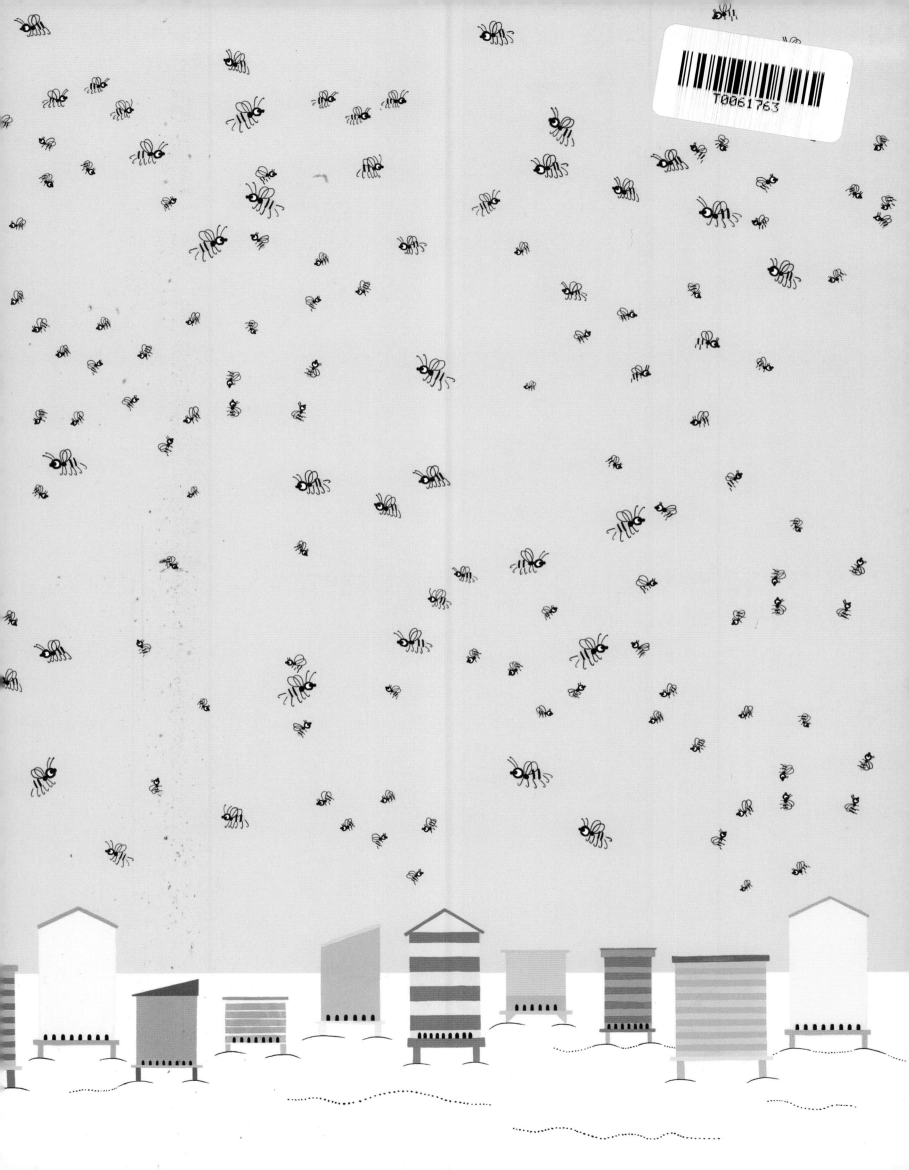

Translated from the French *Mille et une abeilles*

First published in the United Kingdom in 2021 by
Thames & Hudson Ltd, 181A High Holborn, London WC1V 7QX

First published in the United States of America in 2021 by
Thames & Hudson Inc., 500 Fifth Avenue, New York, New York 10110

Original edition © 2020 Actes Sud, Arles
This edition © 2021 Thames & Hudson Ltd, London

British Library Cataloguing-in-Publication Data.
A catalogue record for this book is available from
the British Library

Library of Congress Control Number 2020945388

ISBN 978-0-500-65265-7

Printed in China

Be the first to know about our new releases,
exclusive content and author events by visiting
thamesandhudson.com
thamesandhudsonusa.com
thamesandhudson.com.au

Joanna Rzezak

1001 BEES

T
&H

Mr. Busby is a beekeeper. His garden is filled with beehives.

Beekeepers look after bees and collect the honey that they make.

Beehives don't always stay in the same place. Some beekeepers move their hives to make sure that there are enough flowers nearby for the bees to visit.

Sometimes, fruit growers ask beekeepers to bring hives to their orchards, so the bees can pollinate the trees.

Beekeepers gather the honey from the hives in summer.

From a distance, the hive looks still and quiet, but inside it's buzzing with activity! Bees never stop working. Their hive is very organized and every bee has a job to do.

Most of the bees in a hive are female **worker bees**. Their jobs include cleaning the comb, feeding the larvae, building new combs, guarding the hive and helping to keep it cool, and making honey.

The **queen** is bigger than the other bees in the hive. Her only job is to lay lots of eggs that will grow into new bees. She is always surrounded by a small group of workers, who are called attendants. Their job is to keep her clean and feed her a special food called royal jelly. A queen bee can live for four or five years.

Bees have "pollen baskets" on their back legs. These are special hairy patches that the pollen sticks to.

KEEP AN EYE OUT!
A LITTLE BEE WITH BASKETS FULL OF ORANGE POLLEN ON HER BACK LEGS IS HIDING IN THE OTHER PICTURES IN THIS BOOK. CAN YOU SPOT HER?

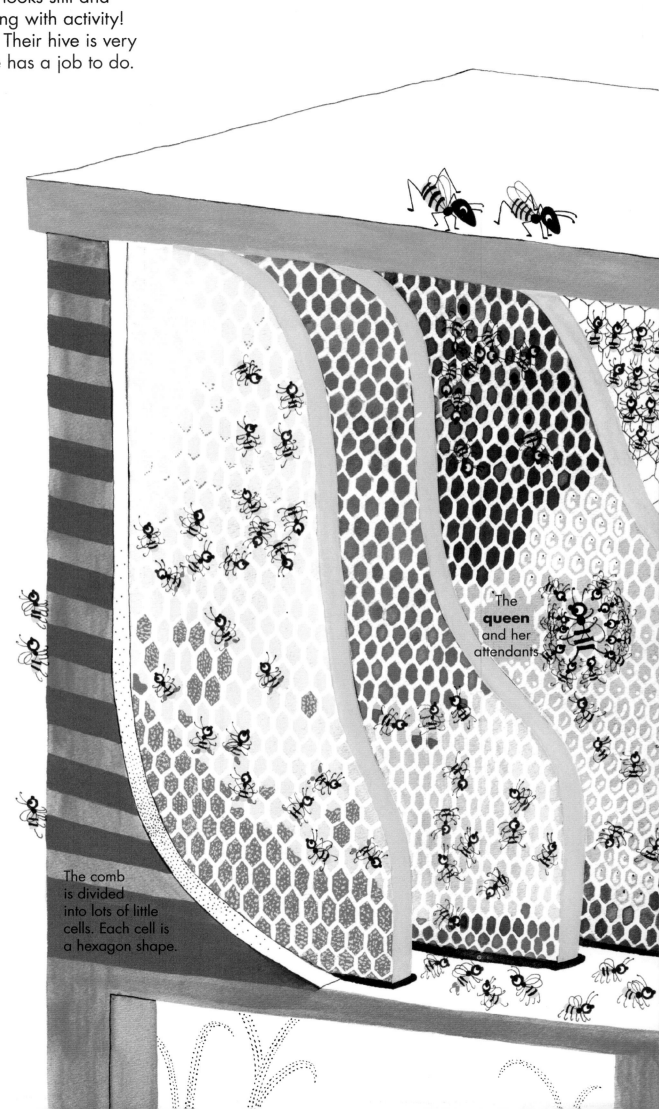

The **queen** and her attendants

The comb is divided into lots of little cells. Each cell is a hexagon shape.

When a bee finds nectar, it comes back to the hive and does a "**waggle dance**" for the other bees. To tell them exactly where the flowers are, it changes the speed and direction of the dance.

Guard bees watch over the entrance to the hive. They make sure that no wasps or bees from other hives get in!

The workers that leave the hive to collect nectar are called **forager bees**. They gather it in a special honey stomach. When they come back, they put the nectar inside the cells of the comb, where it will be turned into honey.

Worker bees begin their working lives by cleaning the combs and feeding the larvae. Then they start looking after the queen, and building new combs. Last of all, they move on to outdoor jobs, like guarding the hive or gathering nectar.

Male bees are called **drones**. Their only job is to mate with the queen, so she can lay more eggs that will grow into new bees.

The queen lays her eggs inside special cells in the comb. Worker bees feed the larvae for a few days. Then they use wax to seal each larva inside its cell.

The larva keeps growing and after 21 days, it chews through the wax and comes out as a fully grown bee.

Builder bees build new cells with wax made by their bodies.

A team of workers stand at the entrance to the hive and flap their wings. This brings air into the hive and keeps it from getting too hot.

In spring, the number of bees in the hive begins to grow. There's not enough space for all of them. This is when bees begin to swarm.

The old queen leaves the hive with some of the young workers. They settle on a branch and form a big hanging swarm.

Scout bees set out to look for a new home for the swarm. They search the nearby area and come back to tell the other bees when they find a good place to live. They do this by doing a dance in the air.

Wait for me, everybody!

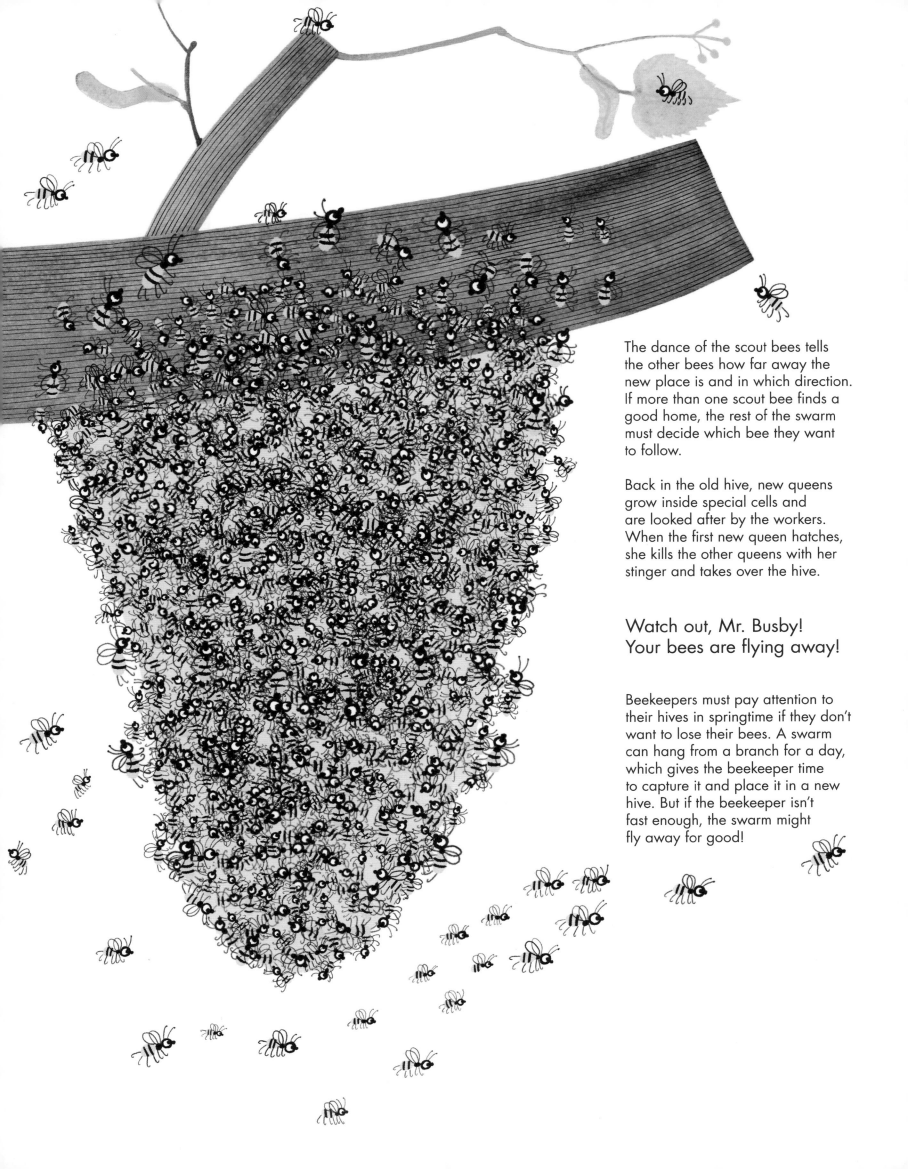

The dance of the scout bees tells the other bees how far away the new place is and in which direction. If more than one scout bee finds a good home, the rest of the swarm must decide which bee they want to follow.

Back in the old hive, new queens grow inside special cells and are looked after by the workers. When the first new queen hatches, she kills the other queens with her stinger and takes over the hive.

Watch out, Mr. Busby! Your bees are flying away!

Beekeepers must pay attention to their hives in springtime if they don't want to lose their bees. A swarm can hang from a branch for a day, which gives the beekeeper time to capture it and place it in a new hive. But if the beekeeper isn't fast enough, the swarm might fly away for good!

Cornflowers

Poppies often grow in fields.
If you shake their round seedpods,
the tiny seeds will come out.

Ants often look after
tiny insects called aphids.
The aphids make a juice
called honeydew,
which ants love to
eat. Ladybirds
(or ladybugs)
love to eat
aphids, so
ants sometimes
have to fight
to protect their
aphid flock!

Field mice eat
insects, seeds and
nuts. They look cute
but they can cause
a lot of damage
to crops!

Silverweed

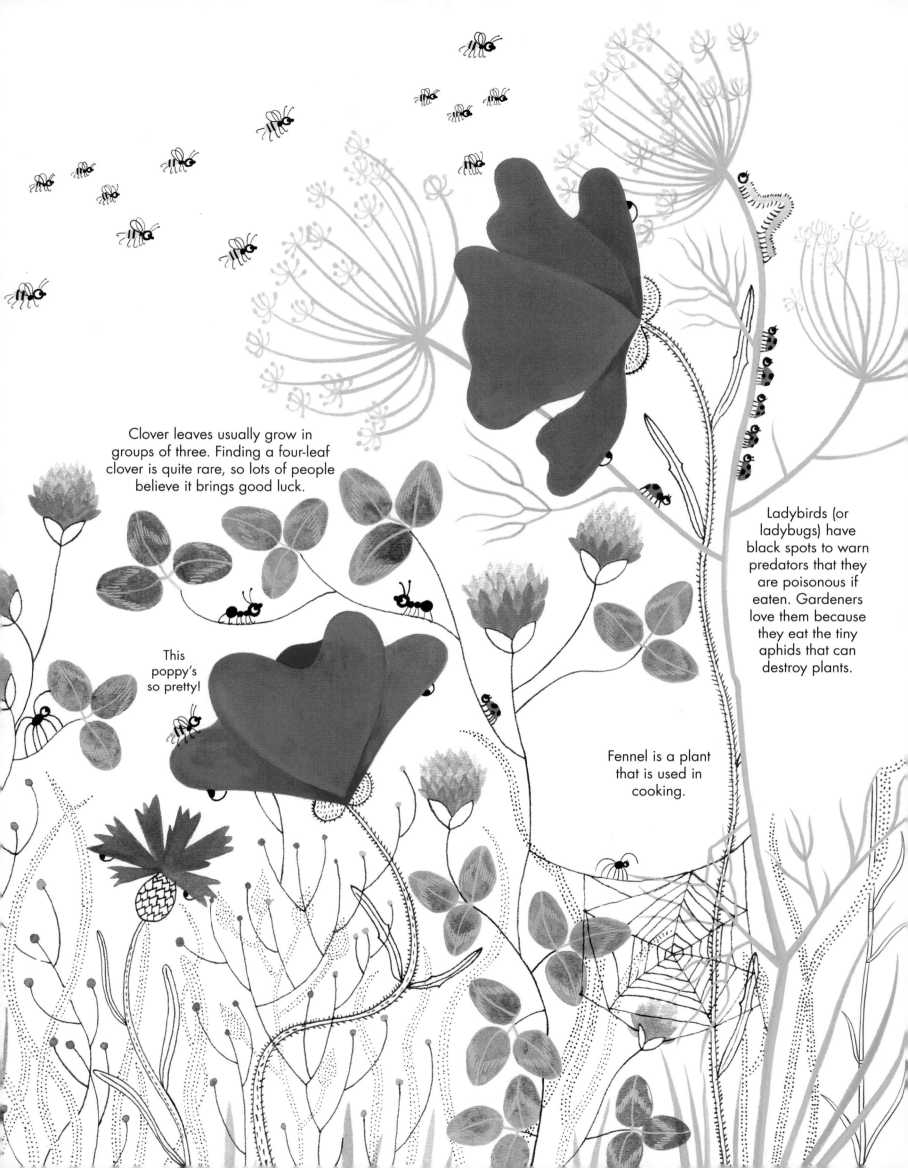

Clover leaves usually grow in groups of three. Finding a four-leaf clover is quite rare, so lots of people believe it brings good luck.

Ladybirds (or ladybugs) have black spots to warn predators that they are poisonous if eaten. Gardeners love them because they eat the tiny aphids that can destroy plants.

This poppy's so pretty!

Fennel is a plant that is used in cooking.

I hope I don't fall and get my feet wet!

The yellow iris often grows in marshy places.

Damselfly

Watch out, nettles can sting you! But they're not all bad. They can also be eaten as a vegetable or used to make a green dye.

A bee can fly 80 km (50 miles) in a day!

The heron uses its long legs to wade in shallow water, looking for food. Its long beak is very good for catching fish.

A marsh is a wetland area where lots of rushes and grasses grow.

The soil is spongy and it's hard to grow crops there.

It's a popular place for birds to live.

The bees fly over a field of wheat.
Soon it will be harvest time.

I'm buzzing
with excitement!

The mustard
plant has
yellow flowers.
Its seeds are
used to make
mustard.

The lark starts
singing before the
sun rises. Being
"up with the larks"
means getting out
of bed early!

Wheat, barley,
oats and rye are
all cereal crops.

Rapeseed
is a plant
that's
harvested
for its oil.

Oats

Many years ago, farmers harvested their crops by hand, using a scythe. Now most farmers use combine harvesters.

Barley is a grain that's often used to feed animals.

Wheat

Leaf bugs

This blue tit is looking for food. It makes its nest in a hollow tree.

No bird will mistake me for its dinner!

Camomile (or chamomile) flowers smell good. They can be dried and used to make tea.

Mint is a leafy green plant with a fresh taste. It's used in toothpaste and chewing gum.

Two toads are hiding among the plants, waiting for insects to eat. They are related to frogs but their skin is thicker and rougher. It stops them from drying out in warm weather.

Onion flowers
are round
and fluffy.

Thyme is
a tasty herb
that's used
in cooking.

Lavender

Listen! The summer air is full of the sound of insects.

Bumblebees are bigger and furrier than honey bees. They don't make honey, but they do an important job, carrying pollen from flower to flower. This helps new flowers to grow.

A bee can fall asleep on a flower! It grabs the flower with its mouthparts and lets its body hang in the air.

The field grasshopper has shorter antennae than the green grasshopper. It chirps by rubbing its leg against its wing.

This nectar is glorious!

Fennel

Morning glory flowers make lots of nectar, so bees love to visit them.

The common green grasshopper sings by rubbing its back leg against the edge of its wing.

The cicada is another kind of chirping insect. It sings using a special organ on its stomach.

The cricket is the insect with the loudest chirp. It can be heard almost half a mile away!

Cherry trees grow beautiful blossoms in spring.

For trees to grow fruit, they need insects to pollinate them. Bees are not the only creatures that do this. Butterflies, wasps, flies and mosquitoes can all carry pollen, and so can some birds. But bees do a big share of the job!

A bee can visit up to 250 flowers in one hour.

This is my 146th flower of the day!

Pollination is the way that plants reproduce. When an insect visits a flower to drink its nectar, it gets pollen on its body. When it moves to another flower, it carries the pollen with it. This fertilizes the plant and makes new seeds grow.

Bullfinch

Bees leave a trail of scent behind them. This helps them tell which flowers they have already visited.

The cherry tree grows cherries in summer. Harvest time is on its way.

Starlings love to eat berries and other fruits. Gardeners and farmers don't like it when they visit!

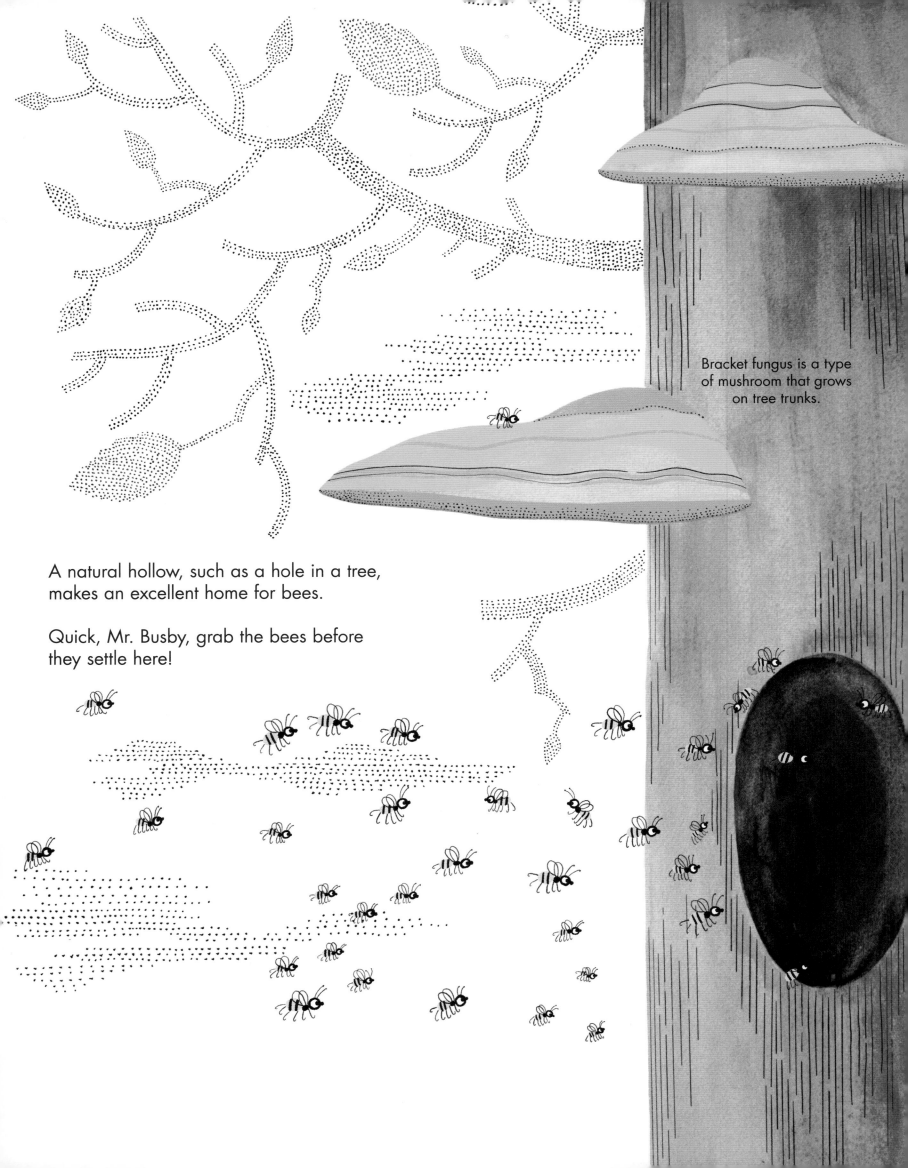

Bracket fungus is a type of mushroom that grows on tree trunks.

A natural hollow, such as a hole in a tree, makes an excellent home for bees.

Quick, Mr. Busby, grab the bees before they settle here!

Squirrels like to make their homes in hollow trees. Their long tails help them to balance when they run and jump along the branches.

This is a strange leaf...

Squirrels also play a part in helping plants to reproduce. They collect acorns, nuts and seeds and store them for the winter. But they often forget where their food stores are, leaving the nuts and seeds to grow into new plants.

Success at last! Mr. Busby
has captured the swarm.

So where are the bees now? They're safe and sound in a brand new hive!

Wow! What a nice new home!

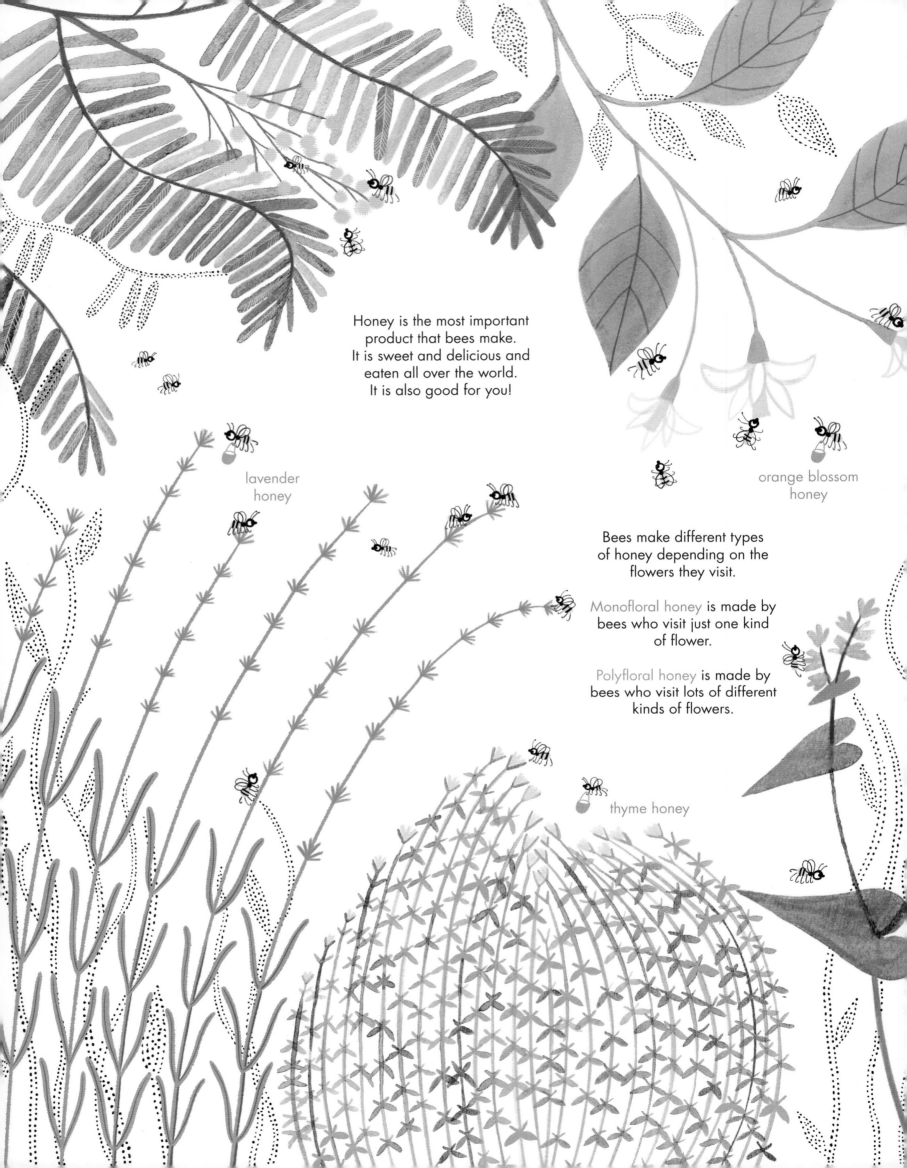

Honey is the most important product that bees make. It is sweet and delicious and eaten all over the world. It is also good for you!

lavender honey

orange blossom honey

Bees make different types of honey depending on the flowers they visit.

Monofloral honey is made by bees who visit just one kind of flower.

Polyfloral honey is made by bees who visit lots of different kinds of flowers.

thyme honey

oak honey

chestnut
honey

buckwheat
honey

acacia
honey

heather
honey

So much
tasty nectar
to enjoy!

wildflower honey

Bees make beeswax using an organ on their
stomach. They use it to build combs for their
honey. Humans often use it to make candles.

Bees also use pollen to make a sticky
substance called propolis or bee glue.
It's used to mend holes in the hive.

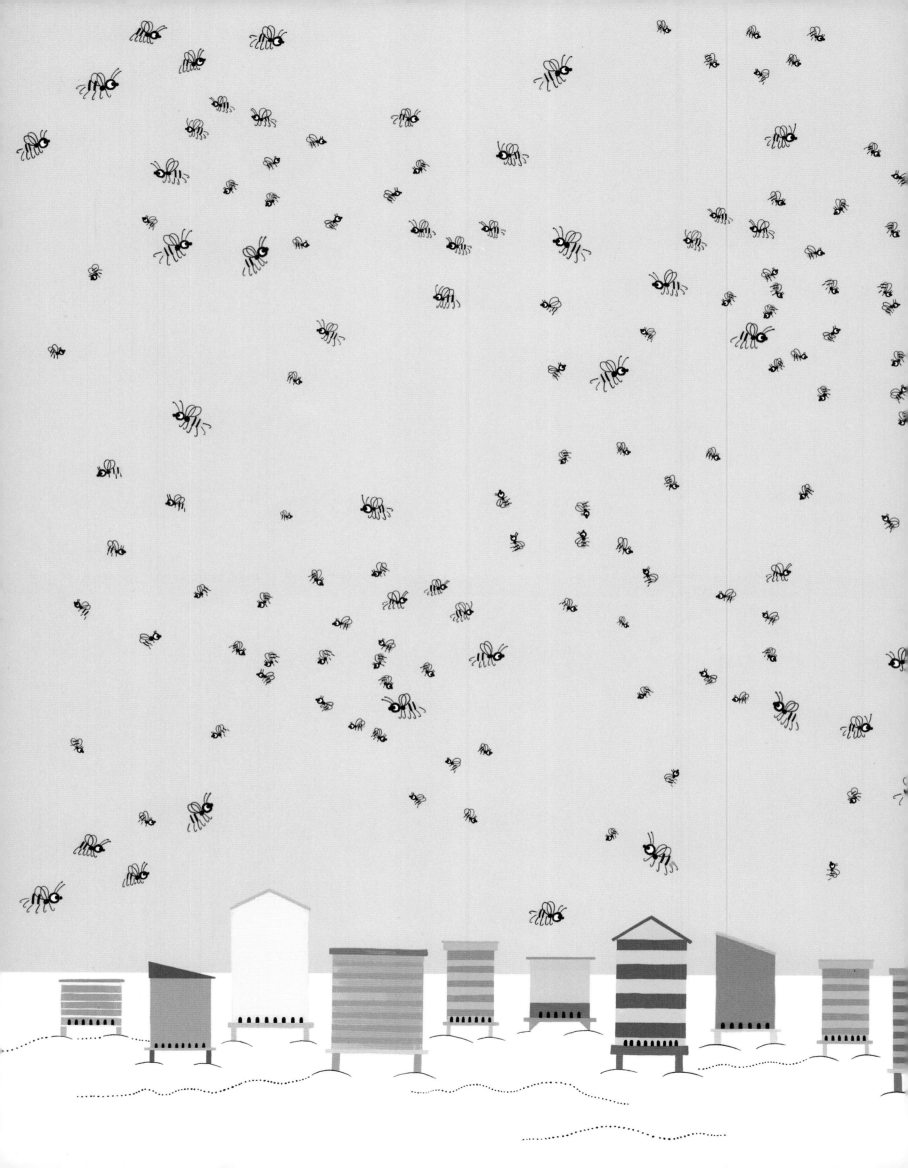